MW01053017

A for ANGELS

A Bible Alphabet

WRITTEN AND ILLUSTRATED BY
LAURIE PARKER

QUAIL RIDGE PRESS

For he shall give his angels charge over thee,
to keep thee in all thy ways.
Psalm 91:11

Acknowledgments:

For helping me continue to create books, thanks first and foremost
as always to Cyndi Clark!

Thank you also to proofreaders Sidney Ruth Morrow,
Brandi Holliman Long, Mama, and Lynn.

Biblical scripture is from the King James Version of the Holy Bible.

Copyright © 2007 by Laurie Parker
ISBN-13: 978-1-934193-48-8 • ISBN-10: 1-934193-48-8

All rights reserved

No part of this book may be reproduced or
transmitted in any form or by any means,
electronic or mechanical, including
photocopying, recording, or by any information
storage and retrieval system, without
permission in writing from the publisher.

Library of Congress Cataloging-in-Publication Data

Parker, Laurie, 1963-
    A for angels : a Bible alphabet / written and illustrated by Laurie Parker.
       p. cm.
    ISBN-13: 978-1-934193-48-8
    ISBN-10: 1-934193-48-8
    1. Bible stories, English. 2. English language—Alphabet—Juvenile
literature. I. Title.
    BS551.3.P36 2010
    235'.3--dc22   2010018263

Printed in South Korea by Tara TPS.
9 8 7 6 5 4 3

QUAIL RIDGE PRESS
P. O. Box 123, Brandon, MS 39043 • 1-800-343-1583
info@quailridge.com • www.quailridge.com

**A**CQUAINT *now thyself with him, and be at peace.* Job 22:21

BEHOLD, *I make all things new.*
Revelation 21:5

COMMIT *thy works unto the LORD, and thy thoughts shall be established.*
Proverbs 16:3

 is for ANGELS
that come from above.

These beings are agents of God's light and love.
The Bible has many astounding accounts
Where angels gave aid, or had news to announce.
From heaven to earth and then back, angels streamed
Upon a grand ladder of which Jacob dreamed.
Even today, angels come to assist.
Be very aware, or their acts will be missed.

AWAKE thou that sleepest, and ARISE from the dead, and Christ shall give thee light.
Ephesians 5:14

A for ANGELS

But the **ANOINTING** which ye have received of him **ABIDETH** in you, and ye need not that any man teach you.   1 John **2:27**

 is for BETHLEHEM.
Long, long ago,

Beams from a star bathed this small town below.
A barn there glowed brightly with beautiful light
Because of a baby boy born there one night.
The animals bowed. Shepherds came to behold.
It's one of the best Bible tales ever told.
This child in a blanket brought God's love to earth,
And that's why believers still honor his birth.

*And he is **BEFORE** all things, and **BY** him*
all things consist.

Colossians 1:17

He hath made every thing **BEAUTIFUL** *in his time: also he hath set the world in their heart, so that no man can find out the work that God maketh from the beginning to the end.* Ecclesiastes 3:11

B for BETHLEHEM

C's for a COAT—
a fine, COLORFUL one

That Jacob of Canaan gave Joseph his son.
He crafted this clothing in which Joseph dressed.
Of all his twelve sons, Jacob loved Joseph best.
The brothers, who coveted what Joseph had,
Conspired to do something cold-hearted and bad.
They ripped Joseph's coat off when he came around
And threw him down into a pit in the ground.
Then, when a trade caravan traveled by,
They sold their own brother and told a cruel lie.
They went to their father with poor Joseph's coat
Which they had dipped into the blood of a goat.
Their father was fooled by this thing they had done.
He thought a wild beast had devoured his son.
But Joseph lived on—now in some other land.
His story continued the way that God planned.

Colossians 2:10   *And ye are **COMPLETE** in him.*

CONSIDER the lilies how they grow; they toil not, they spin not; and yet I say unto you, that Solomon in all his glory was not arrayed like one of these. Luke **12:27**

C for COAT of many COLORS

 is for DANIEL.
He knew divine things.

He deciphered meanings of dreams had by kings.
One ruler named Darius signed a decree:
"All people must pray," it declared, "unto me."
It went on to state those who dared to defy
Would promptly be thrown to the lions to die.
Despite this dire threat, Daniel still disobeyed.
There was but one God to whom this prophet prayed.
His enemies knew this and pushed his arrest.
The king, who liked Daniel, was very distressed.
Duped into drafting this law by those men,
He had to have Daniel put into the den.
"Your God will deliver you," Darius said,
But deep down, the young king was burdened with dread.
So Daniel was shut up with lions all night.
The king ate no dinner and didn't sleep right.
Would Daniel's God save him? The king had such doubt.
At daybreak he dashed to the den and called out,
"Daniel!" he cried. "Are you there? Do you hear?
Were you saved from death by the God you hold dear?"
The king was astounded when Daniel replied.
He'd not been devoured. He called from inside.
He answered the king in a voice clear and strong,
"Oh, King, live forever. I did you no wrong.
God's angel was here. He defended his own.
The lions stayed docile. They left me alone."

*He that **DWELLETH** in the secret place of the most High*
shall abide under the shadow of the Almighty.

Psalm 91:1

He **DISCOVERETH DEEP THINGS** *out of darkness, and bringeth out to light the shadow of death.* Job 12:22

D for DANIEL

's for ELIJAH,
a prophet of old.

He voiced many edicts from God he was told.
While living in hiding some years by a creek,
He got by on bread ravens brought him by beak.
When he was an elderly man, near the end,
He walked with ELISHA, his helper and friend.
A bright, horse-drawn chariot came from on high
To escort Elijah off into the sky.
Elijah left earth, but a part of him stayed
Through spiritual powers Elisha displayed.
Centuries later Elijah was spied
One day on a mountain by Jesus's side.

*For the **EARNEST EXPECTATION** of the creature*
waiteth for the manifestation of the sons of God.
Romans 8:19

ENTER into thy closet, and when thou hast shut thy door, pray to thy Father which is in secret; and thy Father which seeth in secret shall reward thee openly.   Matthew 6:6

E for ELIJAH

 is for FIVE THOUSAND followers FED

With two little fish and just five loaves of bread.
This crowd formed to hear Jesus talk one fine day,
And they became famished. They'd come a long way.
The mindful disciples looked carefully around.
The two fish and five loaves were all that they found.
Christ thanked the young fellow who furnished this fare,
Then offered the Father a thanksgiving prayer.
The food was passed out. All the folks had their fill.
And there were twelve basketfuls left over still.

*Through **FAITH** we understand*
*that the worlds were **FRAMED** by the word of God,*
so that things which are seen were not made
of things which do appear.

Hebrews 11:3

F for FIVE THOUSAND FED

I came FORTH from the FATHER, and am come into the world: again, I leave the world, and go to the Father. John 16:28

's for GOLIATH,
a GIANT from Gath.

His mind-boggling height frightened all in his path.
David, a shepherd boy, stepped up with gall,
"I'll go get that giant—no matter how tall!
Please grant me permission," he said to King Saul.
So armed with a sling, David faced this grave foe
And knocked him clean down to the ground with one blow.
Goliath was giant, but David was greater—
Girded with faith in his God and Creator.

*My **GRACE** is sufficient for thee.*
2 Corinthians 12:9

*Every **GOOD GIFT** and every perfect gift is from above,*
and cometh down from the Father of lights,
with whom is no variableness, neither shadow of turning.
James 1:17

And the *GLORY* which thou gavest me I have *GIVEN* them; that they may be one, even as we are one.   John 17:22

G for GOLIATH the GIANT

 is for HANNAH.
This wife hardly smiled,

For she and her husband could not have a child.
She prayed in the house of the Lord and He heard,
And what she had so hoped to happen occurred.
For heaven sent Hannah a sweet baby boy.
He made her feel happy. He brought her heart joy.
A priest raised the son for whom Hannah had prayed.
This honored a promise to God she had made.

Hebrews 3:15   *Today if ye will **HEAR** his voice,
harden not your hearts.*

For as the **HEAVENS** are **HIGHER** than the earth, so are my ways higher than your ways, and my thoughts than your thoughts. Isaiah 55:9

H for HANNAH

 is for ISAAC,
a doted-on lad—

The only son Sarah and Abraham had.
Isaac means "laughter."
They gave him this name
Because they were both very old
when he came.

Their precious boy grew. Then there came a hard test.
God's voice spoke to Abraham with a request:
"Take your son Isaac, your dearly-loved son,
And go up the mountain—I'll show you which one.
There, at the top, let your sacrifice be
The life of your son. Give him back unto Me."
Abraham barely could fathom this task.
Kill his own child? It was too much to ask!
Men would slay animals back in those days,
Then burn them on altars to offer God praise.
A sheep or a goat or perhaps something wild—
That's what was used for the act—not a child!
But Abraham knew he must trust and obey.
If God wanted Isaac, he'd give him away.
He went with his son up the mountain God chose.
He set up an altar. He placed wood in rows.
He laid his son Isaac on top of the wood.
Clutching a knife, poised and ready he stood.
God's Angel called "Abraham! Abraham! Wait!
Your love for the Lord has been shown to be great.
What you love most in life, you were willing to give.
Do not lay a hand on the lad. Let him live."
Just then, a wild ram captured Abraham's eye.
Its horns were caught up in the bushes nearby.
So Abraham offered the ram up instead.
"You shall be blessed," the Lord's Angel then said.

*The **INWARD** man is renewed day by day.*

2 Corinthians 4:16

I for ISAAC

For the **INVISIBLE** things of him from the creation of the world are clearly seen, being understood by the things that are made.
Romans 1:20

 is for JONAH.
When God told this man

That there was a job he must do, Jonah ran.
He journeyed to Joppa, a town by a bay.
He jumped on a ship there and just sailed away.
A storm came and jostled the boat. The waves roared.
The others blamed Jonah, who'd angered his Lord.
They threw Jonah off and the waves ceased to roll.
Then, GULP! A huge fish swallowed Jonah down whole!
And inside its gigantic belly he stayed.
For three days and nights he was there, and he prayed.
So God gave the jumbo-sized fish a command.
It spit Jonah up safely back on the land.
You can't run from God—that's what Jonah now knew.
He went where God sent him to preach what was true.

John **7:24**
JUDGE *not according to the appearance,*
but judge righteous judgment.

Fulfil ye my **JOY**, that ye be likeminded, having the same love, being of one accord, of one mind.   Philippians 2:2

J for JONAH

A KING,
  an Old Testament king,
            is our

King Nebuchadnezzar. That's tricky to say!
His kingdom was Babylon. His empire grew
When he captured Judah and her people, too.
He ravaged Jerusalem, Judah's main town.
His armies stole treasures then burned the place down.
King Nebuchadnezzar was now in command
Of Jews whom he kidnapped away from their land.
These captives in Babylon felt very sad.
They missed their home country and life they once had.
The king built an idol. He ordered, "Behold!
Kneel to my towering statue of gold!
Worship this idol the way I require,
Or go in the furnace and burn in the fire!"
Three brave, faithful fellows from Judah said, "No.
We worship the true God. He'll save us, we know."
This angered the king and he let out a roar:
"Make the fire hotter now! Seven times more!"
The guards bound the three men who would not comply
And forced them right into the furnace to die.
The heat was so great that it melted the skin
And killed the king's guards who had thrown the three in.
King Nebuchadnezzar stood just out of range.
He stared at the flames. Then, he saw something strange.
For now there were four men inside—not just three.
They walked in the fire! They were loose! And carefree!
The king was amazed and he called with a shout,
"The God that you serve is most high! Now, come out!"
So three men came out, free of soot and not burned.
The fourth was an angel inside, the king learned.

The **KINGDOM** *of God is within you.*

Luke 17:21

KNOCK, *and it shall be opened unto you.* Luke 11:9

K for KING Nebuchadnezzar

 is for LAZARUS.
Maybe you've read

The story of how he was raised from the dead.
This brother of Mary and Martha had died.
His loved ones lamented the loss. How they cried!
Jesus wept also when he learned the news.
A loyal friend in life is a hard thing to lose.
Christ made a request that the men roll away
The large stone that sealed up where Lazarus lay.
"Come forth!" the Lord Jesus then summoned aloud,
And out hobbled Lazarus, still in his shroud.
This man who was dead for four days had come to.
Christ showed there's no limit to what God can do.

*O send out thy **LIGHT** and thy truth:*
***LET** them **LEAD** me.*

Psalm 43:3

Leviticus 19:18   *Thou shalt **LOVE** thy neighbour as thyself: I am the **LORD**.*

L for LAZARUS

 is for MIRACLES,
great acts of God—

Moving, amazing, mysterious, odd...
You just learned how Lazarus had life restored
When he was miraculously raised by the Lord.
And right before that awesome story you learned
Of three men unharmed in a furnace that burned.
Impossible things came to pass through God's might
In more Bible stories like this we can cite.
There's Moses dividing the Red Sea in two,
And manna, a bread sent each morning like dew.
Matthew and Luke give reports of another—
The wonder of Mary becoming a mother.
A baby arrived through a miracle birth
To bring a Messiah's new message to earth.
Men marveled at feats that this Master performed.
He made wine from water and calmed seas that stormed.

*Behold, I show you a **MYSTERY**;*
We shall not all sleep, but we shall all be changed.

1 Corinthians 15:51

*Let this **MIND** be in you, which was also in Christ Jesus:*
Who, being in the form of God,
thought it not robbery to be equal with God.

Philippians 2:5-6

This then is the **MESSAGE** which we have heard of him, and declare unto you, that God is light, and in him is no darkness at all.   1 John 1:5

M for MIRACLES

 is for NOAH,
a name you might know.

A good, upright man, he lived eons ago.
The rest of the people on earth then were bad.
Their nature was evil. It made the Lord sad.
The whole wicked world then so troubled God's heart,
He planned to destroy it and get a new start.
God notified Noah that he would be spared
And gave him instructions on getting prepared.
So Noah worked building a boat called an ark.
He hammered in nails. He worked daily past dark.
He filled it with animals—two of each kind.
The neighbors thought Noah was out of his mind.
But then the rains came, and it poured and it poured.
Noah and family were nestled on board.
The rain fell nonstop—forty days, forty nights.
The water rose up on the ground to great heights.
The flood was worldwide and all living things drowned
Except for the ones on the ark, safe and sound.
The rains finally ceased, but the earth was still wet,
So no one could get off the ark—not just yet.
No dry ground was anywhere near, Noah learned.
He sent out a dove and it quickly returned.
But when he released it again the next week,
It came back this time with a branch in its beak.
The dove had found land! The long nightmare was through!
They came off the ark to begin life anew.
They noticed a rainbow. God sent it to say
He'd never again flood the world in that way.

*Draw **NIGH** to God, and he will draw nigh to you.*

James 4:8

...And have put on the **NEW** man, which is renewed in knowledge after the image of him that created him.   Colossians 3:10

N for NOAH'S ARK

 is for OIL
in a tale told in Kings—

A tale that shows God does omnipotent things.
There once was a widow, alone and upset,
With overdue bills and with outstanding debt.
A man she owed money to ordered she pay
Or else he would come take her two sons away.
She went to Elisha, a prophet admired.
"What do you have you could sell?" he inquired.
The widow replied in a crestfallen tone,
"One vessel of oil. That is all that I own."
"Go borrow some jars," said Elisha. "A lot.
And fill them," he said, "with the oil from your pot."
She borrowed the jars and she started to pour.
Her oil filled one jar, then another, then more.
It poured on and on as God's grace overflowed!
She then sold the oil for the money she owed.

OPEN thou mine eyes,
that I may behold wondrous things out of thy law.
Psalm 119:18

O for Widow's OIL

*Him that **OVERCOMETH** will I make a pillar in the temple of my God, and he shall go no more out.*   Revelation 3:12

P is for PARABLES,
stories that teach.

Jesus used parables when he would preach.
He once told the people a popular one
That's known as the Tale of the Prodigal Son.
A man had two sons who were privileged and blessed.
They'd someday inherit the wealth he possessed.
The youngest said, "Father, I ask you allow
That I have my portion of riches right now."
With money in pocket, this son then left home.
He wanted to play, pursue pleasure, and roam.
In no time he'd spent all the money he brought.
He found himself penniless, poor, and distraught.
He worked feeding pigs. He knew hunger and lack.
He pined for his home, so he finally went back.
Preparing to beg, he had swallowed his pride.
He doubted they'd even permit him inside.
His father, who saw him approach, cried with joy.
He ran out to greet and to kiss his dear boy.
He welcomed his child who returned home ashamed.
"We're having a party!" the father proclaimed.
This story of one parent's love lets us see
The way God the Father accepts you and me.

Psalm 16:11 *Thou wilt show me the **PATH** of life:*
*in thy **PRESENCE** is fullness of joy;*
*at thy right hand there are **PLEASURES** for evermore.*

For he is our *PEACE*, who hath made both one, and hath broken down the middle wall of partition between us.
Ephesians 2:14

P for PARABLE of the PRODIGAL Son

's for a QUEEN
who embarked on a quest.

She came quite a distance to be a king's guest.
She traveled from Sheba with jewels and gold
To meet with a king who was widely extolled.
The king was King Solomon. He was so wise.
The Queen asked him questions. She liked his replies.
Bequeathed both with wisdom and riches galore,
This king proved to be all she'd hoped for and more.

In **QUIETNESS**
and in confidence shall be your strength.
Isaiah 30:15

QUENCH not the Spirit.
1 Thessalonians 5:19

It is the spirit that **QUICKENETH**; the flesh profiteth nothing.   John 6:63

Q for QUEEN of Sheba

 is for RUTH,
a responsible wife.

A book of the Bible is named for her life.
When Ruth's husband died, she was left on her own.
His mother, Naomi, was also alone.
Ruth said to Naomi, "I'm staying with you.
Where you go, I'll go. Where you live, I will, too."
The two then returned to Naomi's homeland
Where romance for Ruth was arranged by God's hand.
Ruth worked in a grain field when harvest time came.
The field was a rich man's. Do you know his name?
The man was called Boaz. He watched Ruth and saw
How loyal she was to her mother-in-law.
Ruth won his respect and he made her his bride.
Naomi came into their home to reside.

REJOICE, and be exceeding glad:
for great is your *REWARD* in heaven.
Matthew 5:12

The Lord **RECOMPENSE** *thy work,*
and a full **REWARD** *be given thee.*   **R**uth 2:12

REMEMBER therefore from whence thou art fallen, and *REPENT*.

Revelation 2:5

R for RUTH

 is for SAMSON,
a man of great strength.

The secret to this
was his hair's longer length.
He fought against Philistines.
they were a clan
Who worshipped an idol,
half fish and half man.

They had Samson bound up one time—tied with rope.
They thought they had won. Samson shattered that hope.
He broke through the thick ropes as if they were string.
He grabbed a mule's jawbone and started to swing.
The stout, sturdy Samson surmounted those foes,
And one thousand troops fell that time to his blows.
The day came when Samson was tricked by a spy—
A Philistine woman who'd captured his eye.
Her name was Delilah and she had been hired
By Samson's arch-rivals, with whom she conspired.
She pleaded with Samson. She begged him each night,
"Tell me your secret! What gives you your might?"
Her whining and wiles finally got him to yield.
"The key is I can't cut my hair," he revealed.
That night Samson slept with his head on her lap.
A man sneaked in silently during the nap.
He shaved Samson's locks off. The haircut was crude.
The Philistines knew he could now be subdued.
So Samson awoke to a dreadful surprise.
His enemies seized him. They gouged out his eyes.
His strength had been sapped when his long hair was shaved.
Now he was their captive, a blind man, enslaved.
The Philistines threw a big party one night.
They ushered in Samson and sneered with delight.
He stood by two columns. He silently prayed,
"Lord God, give me strength one last time as my aid."
He leaned on the columns. He strained hard to shove.
They started to give and the roof shook above.
As Samson recovered his strength from before,
He made the whole building collapse in a roar.
The Philistines there were all instantly killed.
Samson died, too. It was what he had willed.

*If ye **SEEK** him, he will be found of you.*   2 Chronicles 15:2

Be **STILL**, and know that I am God.   Psalm 46:10

S for SAMSON

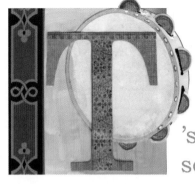

T's for a TOWER
some ancient men planned.

"Let's build something tall!" they exclaimed.
"Something grand!"
They tackled the task. They used bricks laid with tar.
They bragged, "Who needs God? Look how clever WE are!"
The top of their building reached into the sky.
"We'll be high like gods!" was their triumphant cry.
The Lord knew the troubles such pride brings to man,
And so he did something that thwarted their plan.
He mixed up the one, single language they used.
They spoke in new tongues now. Their talk was confused.
Construction was halted with teamwork defeated.
The tower they'd toiled on was never completed.
Their town was called "Babel" from that moment forth.
The people were scattered east, west, south, and north.

*Be ye **TRANSFORMED***
by the renewing of your mind.

Romans 12:2

TRUST in the LORD with all thine heart; and lean not unto thine own understanding. Proverbs 3:5

T for TOWER of Babel

's for the large UPPER ROOM where Christ met

To sup with disciples he'd never forget.
They shared in a Passover meal that was spread
The day of the feast of the unleavened bread.
Christ uttered some meaningful words in that room
When breaking and blessing the bread they'd consume.
"This is my body," he told the twelve men.
We value those words Jesus used way back then.
When passing the cup they would drink from, he said,
"This is my blood, which for many is shed."
Christ knew of the upcoming fate he would meet.
It made this last supper with friends bittersweet.

*God hath made man **UPRIGHT**;*
but they have sought out many inventions.

Ecclesiastes 7:29

U for UPPER ROOM

Therefore have I UTTERED that I UNDERSTOOD not; things too wonderful for me, which I knew not. Job 42:3

V is for VISIONS,
great sights seen by few.

Saint John the Divine saw things God let him view.
Living in exile for spreading God's word,
John was quite old when the visions occurred.
He heard a loud noise like a trumpet that blared.
It came from behind, and John turned and he stared.
By seven gold candlesticks burning aglow,
The Son of God stood with his hair white as snow.
His eyes blazed like fire and his face shone so bright.
His voice was like waters that rush past with might.
He held seven stars. His appearance brought awe.
John fell at the feet of the splendor he saw.
"Do not be afraid," Christ assuringly said,
"The First and the Last, I now live, though once dead."
He told John to write it all down and record
The things he would witness, unveiled by the Lord.
What glories the former disciple was shown!
He visited heaven and viewed a vast throne.
The ONE who sat on it was vividly clear.
A rainbow surrounded the throne in a sphere.
And John saw more visions, both wondrous and odd:
A Lamb, falling stars, many angels of God.
John saw a new heaven and earth come about
Where God dwells forever within, not without.
The visions and trip to the Kingdom John took
Are in Revelation, the Bible's last book.

*This is the **VICTORY** that overcometh the world.*

1 John 5:4

But we have this treasure in earthen VESSELS, that the excellency of the power may be of God, and not of us.
2 Corinthians 4:7

V for VISIONS

's for a WOMAN with whom Jesus talked.

They met at a WELL up to which he had walked.
He asked for a drink—then, an odd thing to do,
For she was Samaritan; he was a Jew.
She wondered just what kind of man he must be.
"Why are you speaking," she asked him, "to me?"
"If you only knew who I AM," he replied,
"You'd ask for the water that I can provide.
The water I give will forever end thirst."
Christ offered these words. The two further conversed.
He knew of her ways—secrets she would withhold.
She saw he was wise like the prophets of old.
"How should one worship?" she asked with eyes wide.
"In SPIRIT and TRUTH," Jesus warmly replied.

WALK *in* **WISDOM**

toward them that are without.

Colossians 4:5

Many, O LORD my God, are thy **WONDERFUL WORKS** which thou hast done.   Psalm 40:5

W for WOMAN at the WELL

Our  is in EXODUS.

Maybe you know
This word means to exit, to leave, or to go.
A book of the Bible is named for this word.
It tells of a massive escape that occurred.
The people of Israel, way back in the past,
Were living in Egypt and very downcast.
As Hebrews, these people were slaves in that land.
Then Moses showed up there to give them a hand.
Moses was whom God had chosen to be
The leader to help set the Israelites free.
With God as his guide, Moses did a brave thing.
He went to the Pharaoh of Egypt, their king.
He told Pharaoh firmly, "You must let them go.
The Lord God of Israel says it should be so."
But Pharaoh refused. He demanded, "Says who?"
He did not believe in the God Moses knew.
So God sent great plagues—fearsome power displays:
Rivers of blood, frogs and flies, pitch black days.
The Pharaoh gave in while the bad plagues would last,
But then they would stop and he'd change his mind fast.
The Pharaoh was stubborn. He had a hard heart.
He still wouldn't let Israel's people depart.
But then came a sign that would cause the most fright.
The Angel of Death called on Egypt one night.
He passed over some homes—the Israelite ones,
But all the Egyptian homes lost first-born sons.
The Pharaoh was anguished. His eldest son died.
"Go Moses! Go now! Take your people!" he cried.
And that's when the Israelites went—while they could.
They gathered their things and left Egypt for good.
That was the Exodus. That's when they fled.
The Lord sent a guide in the sky up ahead.
A pillar of cloud led them forward each day.
At nighttime a pillar of fire showed the way.

I will **EXALT** *him.*   Exodus 15:2

He hath done **EXCELLENT** things.   Isaiah 12:5

X for EXODUS

 is quite simple.
It's for the word "yoke,"
As used in the following truth which
Christ spoke:

*Take my **YOKE** upon you, and learn of me;*
for I am meek and lowly in heart: and
ye shall find rest unto your souls.

Matthew 11:29

's for ZACCHAEUS.
He wasn't too tall,

Nor was this Jericho man liked at all.
A rich tax collector in Biblical days,
He'd made lots of money in dishonest ways.
Big news came to town and he heard people cheer:
"Jesus! The Nazarene! He's coming HERE!"
Zacchaeus was puzzled. Why such a big deal?
He wanted to see the man causing this zeal.
The crowds would be big, and Zacchaeus just knew
A man of his height wouldn't have a good view.
So when the time came, to be able to see,
He climbed up real high in a sycamore tree.
As Jesus passed by just below on his way,
He paused and looked up. He had something to say.
He called to Zacchaeus and ordered, "Come down!
I'm going to stay at your house while in town."
The crowd was surprised when they heard this request.
This sinner was picked to have Christ as his guest?

Zechariah 2:10
Sing and rejoice, O daughter of **ZION***:*
for, lo, I come, and I will dwell
in the midst of thee, saith the LORD.

Be **ZEALOUS** *therefore, and repent.* Revelation 3:19

Z for ZACCHAEUS

Yes, Christ met a sinner
and made him a friend,
And on that sweet note,
we have come to an end.

Daniel 6:26

For he is the living God, and steadfast forever, and his kingdom that which shall not be destroyed, and his dominion shall be even unto

the end.